HA GIANG
VACATION GUIDE 2023

The Ultimate Ha Giang Guide to a
Thrilling Vacation, Everything You Need
to Know, Unveiling Hidden Gems and
Must See Attractions in Ha Giang
Province, Vietnam.

BETTY R CROSS

COPYRIGHT

TABLE OF CONTENTS

COPYRIGHT   1
TABLE OF CONTENTS   3
INTRODUCTION   4
PLANNING YOUR HA GIANG
ADVENTURE   10
NAVIGATING HA GIANG   18
OVERVIEW OF HA GIANG   25
MUST-SEE ATTRACTIONS   31
HIDDEN GEMS   40
ACTIVITIES AND ADVENTURES   46
EATING AND DINING   53
ACCOMMODATION OPTIONS   58
PRACTICAL INFORMATION   63
SAMPLE ITINERARIES   69
GETTING TO KNOW THE LOCALS   75
CONCLUSION   81
APPENDIX   84

INTRODUCTION

In the far north of Vietnam, in Ha Giang Province, time appears to have stopped in the middle of stunning scenery and a wide range of cultural traditions. This part of the book welcomes you to this undiscovered treasure and offers details on why Ha Giang is an essential travel stop. To make your vacation special, we will also show you how to use this complete travel companion successfully.

Welcome to Ha Giang Province

Imagine a place with steep limestone peaks, meandering routes through the mountains, terraced rice fields, and an ethnically diverse tapestry that has endured for millennia. This is the Ha Giang Province, where rich traditions and stunning natural scenery coexist peacefully.

You will be welcomed by the friendly smiles of the locals, many of whom are Hmong, Tay, Dao, and members of other ethnic groups, as you enter Ha Giang. Their particular traditions, attire, and way of life enrich the province's cultural tapestry and foster an environment of authenticity, which is hard to come by in today's society.

There are several geological treasures in the province's rough terrain, including the UNESCO-designated Dong Van Karst Plateau Geopark, which was carved out by rivers and time. Dramatic rock formations, prehistoric fossils, and otherworldly-looking landscapes may be found here.

In addition to its natural wonders, Ha Giang is a haven for outdoor experiences. Ha Giang provides a wide range of options to discover its natural beauty, whether you're an experienced hiker, a motorbike enthusiast, or just looking for a peaceful respite from the rush and bustle of metropolitan life. The province's landscapes are as varied as they are beautiful, offering everything from strenuous climbs through the Ma Pi Leng Pass to peaceful boat excursions on the Nho Que River.

Why Ha Giang Should Be on Your Travel List

For those looking for a genuine and engaging travel experience, Ha Giang is a must-visit since it is not your standard tourist destination. The following are some strong arguments for why Ha Giang ought to be at the top of your trip must-do list:

Untouched Beauty: The landscapes of Ha Giang are mostly unaffected by commercial tourists. You'll discover unspoiled, pure nature that provides a calm and tranquil setting.

Cultural Richness: Rich cultural diversity may be found in Ha Giang. Every community you visit will provide you a different perspective on the customs, way of life, and artistic expression of the surrounding areas.

Adventure Awaits: Ha Giang provides exciting activities for all kinds of explorers, whether you're into motorbiking, trekking, or just exploring off-the-beaten-path locales.

Photographer's Paradise: If you love taking pictures, Ha Giang's sceneries are a photographer's paradise. Every bend in the road presents a brand-new picture-perfect view.

Culinary Highlights: The native cuisine is a pleasant excursion in and of itself, placing a strong focus on fresh, organic ingredients. Don't pass up sampling distinctive foods like "thang co" or sipping locally produced tea.

Warm Hospitality: The inhabitants of Ha Giang are well known for their kind hospitality. You'll often be asked into houses for tea and chat, which can help you make priceless memories.

How to Maximise This Guide

It may be rewarding yet difficult to navigate Ha Giang and find its hidden beauties. To be your dependable travel companion on your wonderful vacation is where this guide comes in.

Plan Your Trip: To get started, make sure you've read the "Getting Ready for Your Ha

Giang Adventure" section and have everything organised. Everything from when to visit Ha Giang to visa requirements and safety advice is covered in this section.

Understand Ha Giang: Read "Ha Giang Province: An Overview" to discover more about the province's history, culture, and the diverse ethnic population that gives it such a special character. The gastronomic pleasures that await you will also be revealed.

Discover Hidden Gems and Must-See Attractions: The areas of this book devoted to Ha Giang's attractions are its most important parts. The section "Must-See Attractions" lists all of the province's famous attractions, while the section "Hidden Gems" reveals the lesser-known attractions that intrepid tourists want to discover.

Plan Your Activities: You may discover suggestions for motorcycling excursions, hiking treks, and cultural activities under "Activities and Adventures." You can use this area to customize your trip based on your interests.

Stay Informed: It's essential to be knowledgeable about everyday issues during your vacation. "Practical Information" provides insights on sustainable travel, health, and communication methods.

Plan Your Itinerary: "Itineraries" offers sample itineraries to help you make the most of your trip whether you're short on time or want a pre-planned excursion.

Connect with Locals: By interacting with the local population, you may learn about the heart and spirit of Ha Giang. The book "Getting to Know the Locals" gives advice on how to treat others with respect and pick up knowledge from them.

You'll be well-prepared to start your Ha Giang journey by following these instructions. Ha Giang Province is certain to create a lasting impression on your heart and spirit, whether you're a solitary traveler, a couple searching for a romantic getaway, or a family seeking an edifying experience.

PLANNING YOUR HA GIANG ADVENTURE

To guarantee a hassle-free and enjoyable trip to Ha Giang, it is important to make arrangements before leaving. We'll provide you advice on the best times to visit Ha Giang, visa and entrance procedures, what to bring, and important safety precautions in this area.

Ideal Time to Go to Ha Giang

The ideal time to visit Ha Giang will mainly depend on your interests and what you intend to see or do there since its attractiveness changes with the seasons:

Spring (March to April): The season of blossoming flower and lush vegetation. Water begins to flood the terraced rice fields, resulting in a colorful scene. Trekking and other outdoor activities are perfect because of the beautiful weather.

Summer (May to August): Ha Giang's summers may be hot and muggy, with sporadic rain. Be ready for soggy circumstances even though the scenery is still lush since it is the rainy season right now. The greenest sceneries may be seen at this time.

Fall (September to November): Fall is regarded as the best season to visit Ha Giang. The sky is often clear, the rice fields become golden, and the temperature drops. Trekking and photography are the best this season.

Winter (December to February): The winter in Ha Giang may be chilly, particularly in the highland regions. In higher altitudes, snowfall is prevalent. For individuals who like a calmer environment and don't mind the cold, this season is ideal.

When selecting your vacation dates, take into account your own interests and the experiences you want to have. It's a good idea to check the forecast before your journey since Ha Giang's weather may be erratic.

Entry Requirements & Visas

It's crucial to comprehend Vietnam's admission regulations and visa requirements before traveling to Ha Giang. Here is a quick summary:

Visa Exemption: For brief visits in Vietnam, several nationalities are not required to get a visa. However, some exemptions have certain requirements, so it's important to see whether you meet them.

Visa on Arrival: You may apply for a visa on arrival (VOA) before your travel if you are not exempt from needing a visa. Typically, this procedure entails receiving a letter of pre-approval before having your visa stamped at one of Vietnam's international airports.

E-visa: For certain nations, Vietnam also provides an electronic visa (e-visa) application procedure. You may apply for a visa online and get it instantly.

Embassy/Consulate: You may apply for a visa at the Vietnamese embassy or consulate in your home country if you'd rather have it in hand before departing.

Make sure your passport is current and has at least six months remaining on it after the date you want to travel. Make sure you are prepared for your trip by double-checking the regulations unique to your nationality.

Packing Necessities

Being well-prepared for diverse activities and weather situations will improve your Ha Giang vacation. Here is a list of necessities to think about bringing:

Clothing

- For the warmer months, wear clothing that is light and breathable.
- Dress in layers during colder months.
- For rainy days, use a waterproof jacket or poncho.
- Sturdy hiking boots or grippy, comfy walking shoes.
- For sun protection, use a hat, sunglasses, and sunscreen.

Gear & Apparatus

- A daypack or backpack for carrying necessities on hikes and other excursions.
- A voltage converter and a travel adaptor, if necessary.
- Power bank for charging your electronics.
- For gadgets and valuables, use dry bags or water-resistant pouches.

Safety & Health

- A first aid kit with bandages and necessary drugs.
- Anti-malarial medicine and insect repellent (if going to a rural location).
- Reusable water bottle and water purification technique (take purification pills or a filter into consideration).

Documentation

- Paperwork for visas and passports.
- Important papers should be copied or digitally saved (apart from the originals).
- Contact details, as well as travel insurance coverage.

Miscellaneous

- Cash (Vietnamese Dong) and Payment options like cards (ATMs may not be available in rural places) .
- For communication, use a local SIM card or international roaming.
- Map or travel manual for Ha Giang.
- Using a travel cushion and earplugs will make lengthy trips more pleasant.

To make your trip more pleasant, remember to pack less. The terrain in Ha Giang might be difficult, so being equipped properly will guarantee that you are ready for any eventualities.

Safety Advice

Even though Ha Giang is a beautiful place, you must put safety first while you are there:

Road Safety: If you want to ride a motorcycle to tour Ha Giang, make sure you have the required riding experience, put on a helmet, and abide by all traffic laws. Be careful since the roads might be narrow and twisty.

Weather Awareness: Keep up with the forecast, particularly if you're going on a hike or engaging in other outside activities. Be prepared for unforeseen weather changes.

Local Customs: Respect the traditions and practices of the local ethnic groups. Before taking pictures of individuals, get their consent and be sensitive to local norms.

Health Care: Drink plenty of water, particularly when trekking, and use care when consuming native food and water. Carrying your own water purifying system is advised.

Travel Insurance: Make sure you have adequate travel insurance that covers evacuation in the event of a medical emergency.

Emergency Contacts: Become familiar with the local authorities and medical agencies' emergency contact numbers.

Solo Travelers: Solo travelers should inform someone of their route and anticipated return times if they are traveling alone.

Responsible Travel: Travel responsibly by reducing your environmental effects, properly disposing of your garbage, and interacting politely with locals to help their communities.

You will have a safe and delightful trip in Ha Giang by paying attention to these safety precautions and coming prepared. This will allow you to fully experience the region's natural beauty and cultural diversity while maintaining your safety all along the way. With the proper planning, Ha Giang awaits, and your trip will be nothing short of remarkable.

NAVIGATING HA GIANG

It's essential to comprehend the topography of this province, the accessible modes of transportation, and how to manage your funds while touring before you go on your journey to Ha Giang. To aid you in navigating Ha Giang successfully, we will provide you a thorough explanation of these factors in this section.

Overview of Ha Giang's Geography

In the extreme north of Vietnam, in the isolated and hilly Ha Giang Province, there are shared borders with China to the north and west. The province's distinctive terrain has a big impact on the breathtaking vistas and potential difficulties tourists can run across.

Mountains & Peaks: With heights ranging from 200 meters to over 2,400 meters above sea level, the province is mostly made up of limestone mountains and peaks. A UNESCO-recognized site, the Dong Van Karst Plateau Geopark is well known for its impressive rock formations and historical geological characteristics.

Rivers & Valleys: Several rivers, including Qthe Gam River and Nho Que River, meander through the valleys, fostering agriculturally productive regions and enhancing the picturesque splendor of the province.

Ethnic Groups: There are many different ethnic groups in Ha Giang, and they all live in different valleys and hilly areas. This variety adds to the province's diverse cultural fabric.

Challenging Terrain: Traveling to Ha Giang may be difficult due to the area's steep topography. Because of landslides and floods, several locations may be inaccessible during the rainy season owing to narrow, twisting roads.

It is crucial to comprehend the topography of Ha Giang since it will affect the mode of transportation you choose and the routes you take to see this gorgeous province.

Options for Transportation

Given its rough terrain, getting around Ha Giang may be an experience in and of itself. The main modes of transportation for moving across the province are as follows:

Motorbike: To freely explore Ha Giang, many tourists choose to hire motorbikes. It allows for adaptability and access to distant locations. However, steep routes might be difficult, so be sure you have the required riding skills and are using safety equipment, such as helmets.

Private Car or Taxi: You may rent a private car or taxi if you'd like a more relaxing and less strenuous choice. Travelers who wish to take in the view without the stress of driving will find this to be excellent.

Public Bus: Major cities and settlements in Ha Giang are connected by public buses. Although they are a cost-effective choice, private transportation could provide more comfort and convenience.

Shared Mini-Vans: Some routes in Ha Giang are served by shared mini-Vans. They provide shared transportation with a small group of people and are a mid-range choice between public buses and private autos.

Trekking & Hiking: Walking and trekking are popular forms of transportation in Ha Giang, particularly in rural regions. You may get a unique view of the region with the help of guided hiking trips.

Boat: Boat trips are offered in various locations, such as the Nho Que River. This is a beautiful approach to see the area from a new angle.

Planning your transportation in advance is crucial, taking into account your comfort level, spending limit, and the destinations you wish to visit. Always check the most recent updates and conditions before starting a travel since road conditions may change at any time.

Currency & Banking Locally

Because of the province's isolated regions and the potential lack of ATMs and banking facilities, managing your money while on an expedition in Ha Giang needs some planning. What you need to know is as follows:

Currency: Vietnamese Dongs (VND) are the nation of Vietnam's official currency. For modest purchases, it's a good idea to have some VND on hand in cash since rural locations cannot take many credit cards.

ATMs: While there are ATMs in large cities like Ha Giang City and Dong Van, they do not always work well, and you can run into a cash shortage. When you have access to ATMs in bigger cities like Hanoi or Haiphong, it is wise to withdraw adequate cash beforehand.

Credit Cards: In major towns, several hotels, restaurants, and businesses take credit cards; but, you shouldn't solely depend on them. Always have some cash on hand in case of an emergency.

Currency Exchange: Compared to larger cities, Ha Giang does not provide as many currency exchange services. It is preferable to change money before traveling or in bigger cities like Ha Giang City.

Budgeting: Carefully plan your spending, taking into account your lodging, food, transportation, and activities. It's a good idea to have some cash on hand as well as a travel card in case of emergencies.

Local Markets: You may purchase a wide range of things at local markets in Ha Giang, including fresh fruit, handicrafts, and traditional apparel. These markets favor cash as a form of payment.

Tipping: Although not required in Vietnam, tipping is often appreciated. It's customary to round up the check-in restaurants, and it's appropriate to tip drivers and tour guides for exceptional service.

Safety Advice: Exercise caution while handling cash in public to prevent unwarranted attention. Put your valuables in a concealed pouch or money belt for security.

You will better manage your money and enjoy your trip without worrying about money if you prepare for the banking and currency realities of Ha Giang. When traveling to rural areas, always have some cash on hand in case of emergency.

For a successful and pleasurable experience in this alluring province, it is essential to have a solid understanding of the terrain, transportation alternatives, and financial concerns of Ha Giang. With this information, you may make travel plans, choose the best method of transportation for your requirements, and make sure you have enough money to have a memorable trip to Ha Giang.

OVERVIEW OF HA GIANG PROVINCE

Understanding Ha Giang's history, culture, and the variety of its people is crucial if you want to enjoy and fully immerse yourself in everything that it has to offer. We will provide you a thorough description of Ha Giang's history, culture, and ethnic variety in this area, as well as information about the delicious local food you may sample while you're here.

History and Culture of Ha Giang

History: The history of Ha Giang Province stretches back thousands of years. Ancient temples, stone fortifications, and the remains of former dynasties all attest to its historical importance. Here are some significant historical details:

- ***Ancient Trade Routes:*** Ha Giang served as a crossroads for trade and cultural exchange thanks to its advantageous position along old trade routes that linked Vietnam and China. It was a component of the storied Tea Horse Road, a system of commercial routes used to transport tea and other items.

- **Chinese Rule:** Throughout history, Ha Giang was ruled by the Chinese, which had an impact on its culture and architecture. Numerous historical sites in the province are witnesses to this time.

- **French Colonial Influence:** Ha Giang was governed by the French during the period of French colonization. This period had an impact on local culture and left remnants of European architecture.

Culture: The culture of Ha Giang is a fusion of local customs, influences from surrounding nations, and the tenacity of its several ethnic groups. Important cultural elements include:

- **Festivals & Celebrations:** Several festivals, often related to agricultural cycles and customs, are held across the province. One such occasion is the "Nao Cong" festival, which honors the beginning of spring. Check the local calendar to see if any festivals are happening while you are there.

- **_Traditional Crafts:_** Ha Giang is well-known for its traditional crafts, which include weaving, embroidery, and silverwork. In local markets, you may buy exquisitely made jewelry and fabrics.

- **_Traditional Clothing:_** Ha Giang's ethnic groups have unique traditional clothes with elaborate patterns and vivid colors. You could have the opportunity to try some on during your stay. The attire expresses the cultural character of each tribe.

- **_Music & Dance:_** Ha Giang's cultural legacy is greatly influenced by traditional music and dance. You could see entertaining performances highlighting the area's many musical traditions.

The Ethnic Diversity of Ha Giang

The astounding ethnic variety of Ha Giang is one of its most notable features. There are many different ethnic groups living in the province, each with its own language, traditions, and way of life. The following are some of the well-known ethnic groups you'll run into:

Hmong: One of Ha Giang's main ethnic groups is the Hmong. Their beautiful needlework and traditional attire are well-known. The Hmong are found in many of the province's communities.

Tay: The Tay ethnic group is renowned for their stilt homes and fishing customs. In Tay communities, you may take in their distinctive architectural aesthetic and delight in their warmth.

Dao: The Dao ethnic group is distinguished for its mastery of herbal medicine and its red turbans. Views of the Dao people's rich cultural customs may be obtained by visiting Dao communities.

Nung: The Nung are famous for their tea farming. In Nung villages, you may visit tea farms and learn how tea is processed.

Lo Lo: The Lo Lo people are one of Ha Giang's smaller ethnic groupings. They are recognized for their distinctive practices, black attire, and hairpins. The Lo Lo communities may be visited to learn more about their unique way of life.

Pho Lu: The iron forging prowess of the Pho Lu people is well recognized. You may see their workmanship in action and discover more about their age-old metalworking methods.

Pu Peo: The Pu Peo people are renowned for their woodcarving abilities and have a strong oral history. Pu Peo communities are home to beautiful wood sculptures.

One of the joys of visiting Ha Giang is learning about the many customs of these ethnic tribes. Respect their customs and interact with locals to learn more about their way of life.

The history and culture of northern Vietnam are all well-explored in Ha Giang Province. It attracts tourists looking for an authentically immersed experience because of its fascinating history, many ethnic populations, and delectable cuisine. Make sure you interact with the locals, indulge in some local food, and appreciate the distinctive customs that make Ha Giang what it is.

MUST-SEE ATTRACTIONS

The province of Ha Giang is a place of unmatched natural beauty and cultural diversity. It has become a must-visit location for tourists looking for real experiences because of its distinctive landscapes and thriving towns. The stunning beauty and rich cultural variety of Ha Giang are on display at five must-see destinations that we shall discuss in this part.

Quan Ba Twin Mountains

Location: Quan Ba District, Ha Giang Province

As you approach Ha Giang Province from the south, the Quan Ba Twin Mountains, popularly referred to as "The Fairy Bosom," greet you. This scene, with its two limestone peaks rising steeply from the valley below, is intriguing and seems almost unearthly.

Reasons to Visit Quan Ba Twin Mountains

Scenic Beauty: One of Ha Giang's most recognizable vistas is provided by the Quan Ba Twin Mountains. Particularly around the time when the fields are being harvested for rice, when they become golden, the contrast between the two towering peaks and the lush green valley is truly magnificent.

Cultural Significance: Hmong and Dao populations in the area revere the mountains as holy places. Visit adjacent communities to discover the cultures and traditions that are intertwined with the local environment.

Photography: If you love taking pictures, this place is a photographer's paradise. Your photos will have more depth and drama due to the shifting light throughout the day.

Hiking: For even more spectacular sights, trek to viewpoints. The majority of people can complete the trek since it is not too difficult.

Local Markets: Go to the nearby Quan Ba Sunday Market to meet the people and buy handcrafted products and ethnic attire.

Dong Van Karst Plateau Geopark

Location: Dong Van District, Ha Giang Province

One of Vietnam's most amazing geological marvels, the Dong Van Karst Plateau Geopark is a UNESCO World Heritage Site. Ancient fossils, unusual rock formations, and geological history may all be found there in plenty.

Why Visit Dong Van Karst Plateau Geopark

Geological Marvels: Explore a landscape that has been formed by geological processes over millions of years with Geological Marvels. Admire the limestone structures, vast gorges, and fossilized reefs that reveal details about Earth's past.

Ha Giang Stone Plateau: This region is often known as the "Ha Giang Stone Plateau," and it is renowned for its large tracts of stony landscape scattered with brilliant flora.

Ethnic Villages: Several ethnic minorities, including the Hmong, Dao, and Tay, have homes in the geopark. Engage with the welcoming folks and experience their way of life.

Lung Cu Flag Tower: The geopark's Lung Cu Flag Tower, which marks Vietnam's northernmost point, is situated there. For sweeping views of the surroundings, ascent to the summit.

Ma Pi Leng Pass: The famed Ma Pi Leng Pass, a breathtaking mountain route that provides some of the most spectacular vistas in the area, is accessible from the geopark.

Ma Pi Leng Pass

Location: Meo Vac District, Ha Giang Province

The famed Ma Pi Leng Pass, often known as the "King of Mountain Passes," runs through the Dong Van Karst Plateau Geopark and is a breathtaking path. It's more than simply a route; it's a journey through breathtaking surroundings.

Reasons to Visit Ma Pi Leng Pass

Spectacular Views: The pass provides some of Ha Giang's most spectacular panoramic vistas. Unparalleled views of the nearby mountains and the Nho Que River may be had from the twisting road perched on the rocks.

Adventure & Thrills: If you're looking for adventure, traveling across the Ma Pi Leng Pass by car or on foot is a thrilling experience. The exhilaration is increased by the winding, steep route.

Photographing: Capture the landscape's untamed beauty. There is no better time to be here with a camera than at sunrise or sunset.

Local Life: Ethnic minority populations may be seen going about their everyday lives along the route. To learn about their culture, stop and engage with them.

Hiking: The region around the pass has hiking routes that you may use to explore on foot and find undiscovered treasures.

Lung Cu Flag Tower

Location: Lung Cu Commune, Dong Van District, Ha Giang Province.

The Lung Cu Flag Tower is a testimony to Vietnam's territorial integrity and a representation of Ha Giang's northernmost point. The tower, which is positioned atop Dragon Mountain, provides sweeping views of the surrounding area.

Reasons to Visit Lung Cu Flag Tower

Cultural Significance: Vietnamese unity and geographical integrity are symbolized by the flag tower. It is a historical landmark and a source of pride for the country.

Amazing Views: Climb the tower to get sweeping panoramas over the borderlands. You can see all the way to China on a clear day.

Ethnic Communities: A variety of ethnic groups, including the Hmong and Tay, call the Lung Cu region home. Discover the cultures and communities in the area.

Unique Topography: The area around Lung Cu is noted for its terraced farms, undulating hills, and traditional agricultural methods. It is a serene and lovely area in Ha Giang.

Hoang Su Phi Terraced Fields

Location: Hoang Su Phi District, Ha Giang Province

The Hoang Su Phi Terraced Fields are evidence of the inventiveness of the locals, who over many years carved the mountain slopes into exquisite rice terraces. These terraces are stunning to look at in addition to being useful.

Reasons to Visit Hoang Su Phi Terraced Fields

Beautiful Scenery: During the planting and harvesting seasons, when the fields are submerged in or glowing with maturing rice, the terraced fields are a visual marvel.

Photography Paradise: Photographers will have many opportunities to capture the scenery, which varies in color and texture throughout the year, in this paradise for photography.

Cultural Connection: Interact with local ethnic groups, such as the Nung, La Chi, and Dao people who have been cultivating these fields for decades. Find all about their farming customs and practices.

Hiking: If you want to fully experience this alluring setting, there are hiking paths nearby that take you through the terraced fields.

Local Markets: Visit the vibrant local markets in cities like Hoang Su Phi to learn about local culture and buy one-of-a-kind gifts.

In addition to being a scenic treat, visiting the Hoang Su Phi Terraced Fields offers an opportunity to interact with the rich agricultural history and ethnic cultures of Ha Giang.

These five must-see sites in Ha Giang provide a window into the region's many topographies, peoples, and cultures. Ha Giang has something remarkable to offer, whether you're an adventure enthusiast, a cultural adventurer, or a nature lover. Take your time to appreciate this extraordinary place's beauty and genuineness.

HIDDEN GEMS

Despite the undeniable beauty of Ha Giang's well-known sites, there is a whole universe of undiscovered treasures just waiting to be found by adventurous visitors. In this section, we'll let you in on some of the province's best-kept secrets, including remote communities, undiscovered natural beauties, and memorable cultural encounters.

Off-the-Beaten-Path Villages

Several villages in Ha Giang are not on the usual tourist itineraries, giving visitors the chance to see real rural life and the many cultures of the area.

Pho Cao Village: A hidden treasure inhabited by the Hmong people and is tucked away high in the highlands. The community provides peace and stunning terraced field views.

Nam Dam Village: A tranquil location where you can see typical Tay stilt homes and learn about their distinctive customs. It is tucked away in the Dong Van Karst Plateau Geopark.

Pho Bang Village: Pho Bang Village is well-known for its intact French colonial architecture and is a picturesque hamlet close to the Chinese border. Take a stroll through the cobblestone streets and take in the ambiance of a bygone era.

Thien Huong Village: Thien Huong Village, in the Hoang Su Phi District, has terraced fields that are just as stunning as those in Sa Pa, but see less tourism. A peaceful location for photography.

Tha Village: Tha Hmong people, who are renowned for their unique clothes and handicrafts, live in this outlying Hmong hamlet, which can only be reached by foot travel. Tha Village provides an insight into the Hmong people's traditional way of life.

Unexplored Natural Wonders

The natural beauty of Ha Giang is not limited to its well-known attractions. Here are a few undiscovered natural wonders that offer exciting new experiences:

Tu San Canyon: As the "Grand Canyon of Vietnam," Tu San Canyon is a well-kept secret that may be found in the Meo Vac District. The canyon offers fantastic trekking options with its high cliffs and flowing river.

Quyet Tien Hot Springs: These natural hot springs, which are found in Quyet Tien Commune, are great for unwinding. They are a wonderful hidden paradise surrounded by thick flora.

Kho My Cave: This undiscovered wonder of the Dong Van Karst Plateau Geopark is home to amazing limestone structures and an underground river. It is a thrilling adventure to delve deeper into.

Nam Dan Woodland: This unspoiled woodland is a great place to see birds and other animals. It is a secret haven for nature lovers because of the lush canopy and unspoiled surroundings.

Nam Ty Valley: Nam Ty Valley is a lesser-known beauty with terraced crops surrounded by thick trees, hidden deep inside the Hoang Su Phi District. It's a serene setting where you may escape the outside world.

Experiences from Diverse Cultures

The chance to partake in unusual cultural experiences that are often off the beaten tourist path is one of the most gratifying parts of vacationing in Ha Giang.

Homestays with Ethnic Communities: Staying at homestays allows you to experience the friendliness and hospitality of the ethnic minority groups in Ha Giang. Not only will you partake in customary meals, but you'll also take part in everyday activities and cultural interactions.

Traditional Festivals: Be on the lookout for regional holidays, which are often observed with vibrant parades, music, and dancing. These occasions provide a glimpse into the region's diverse cultural heritage.

Cultural Workshops: Workshops that teach traditional skills including weaving, needlework, and blacksmithing are available in several areas. It's a practical method to appreciate the abilities of regional craftspeople.

Participate in Rituals: If you have the chance, take part in regional rites and rituals, such as weddings or festivals. You'll learn more about the people's traditions and beliefs.

Morning Marketplaces: Check out the marketplaces that are held in several communities in the early morning hours. Locals flock to these crowded marketplaces to sell items, and they provide a real look into everyday life.

Local Music & Dance: Enjoy traditional performances of local music and dance. The vivid rhythms and colorful costumes are a monument to the region's cultural variety.

Hmong New Year: If your visit coincides with the Hmong New Year (typically in November or December), don't miss the opportunity to see this vivid festival, replete with traditional dress and energetic celebrations.

Exploring these undiscovered attractions in Ha Giang will not only provide you with unforgettable experiences, but it will also provide you the chance to help out the less well-known local populations. Remember to show respect for regional customs and traditions; it's an honor to be permitted access to these remote areas of Ha Giang's culture and environment.

ACTIVITIES AND ADVENTURES

Adventurers and lovers of nature may both enjoy Ha Giang Province. There are a variety of activities that offer remarkable experiences, including thrilling motorcycle excursions, taxing hikes, immersing homestays, and amazing photographic possibilities. We'll dig into the wide variety of activities and experiences in Ha Giang in this part.

Motorbike Tours

Ha Giang Loop: Traveling on the renowned Ha Giang Loop is a once-in-a-lifetime experience. The most attractive regions of the province, including terraced farms, rocky mountains, and tranquil valleys, arc all passed through on this epic motorcycle adventure. The circle normally includes Meo Vac, Quan Ba, Yen Minh, Ha Giang City, and Quan Ba. You'll have plenty of chances to stop for photographs and encounters with people, and the steep mountain roads and hairpin turns will give you an adrenaline boost.

Ma Pi Leng Pass: The Ha Giang Loop's Ma Pi Leng Pass is a standout feature. The Nho Que River meandering through the valley below may be seen magnificently from this high, twisting mountain pass. It's a must for every motorcycle fan and a great place to get breath-taking pictures.

Off-the-Beaten-Path Routes: If you're looking for less-traveled routes, you may want to look into the system of isolated roads that branch off the main loop. These routes may take you to undiscovered settlements, stunning natural settings, and interactions with ethnic minority groups.

Multi-day Tours: Join multi-day motorcycle trips that take you right to the heart of Ha Giang for a thorough experience of the province. These trips often involve homestays, excursions to cultural attractions, and interactions with the local population.

Trekking and Hiking Routes

Dong Van Karst Plateau Geopark: The Dong Van Karst Plateau Geopark provides a wide range of hiking and trekking activities. You may trek to overlooks that provide expansive views of the plateau, explore the region's distinctive limestone formations, and visit nearby settlements.

Nam Son Cave Trek: A hidden treasure encircled by beautiful woods and limestone peaks, Nam Son Cave is accessible by a journey close to Dong Van. The stalactites and stalagmites in the cave are known for their beauty.

Lung Khuy Cave Trek: This journey takes you to Lung Khuy Cave, a natural marvel with a towering entrance and an intriguing interior filled with unique formations. It is situated in the Hoang Su Phi District. Hiking through woodlands and terraced fields is required for the trek.

Trek to Hidden Villages: Arrange excursions to remote, mountainous ethnic minority settlements. These hikes provide chances to interact with local people, see traditional agricultural methods, and take in the tranquility of far-flung regions.

Climbing Ma Pi Leng Peak: Climbing Ma Pi Leng Peak is a difficult activity best left to experienced hikers and climbers. Awe-inspiring panoramic views of the surrounding peaks and valleys are available from the top.

Homestays & Local Experiences

Homestays: A cultural immersion unlike any other may be had by staying in a house of an ethnic minority. Living with local families will allow you to interact with them regularly and learn about their culture. It's a chance to make real friendships and enduring memories.

Cooking Classes: Many homestays provide cooking lessons where guests may learn how to make regional cuisine using traditional recipes. Enjoy meals with your hosts while savoring Ha Giang's delights.

Agricultural Experiences: Participate in agricultural activities with the neighborhood communities. You may assist with rice planting, crop harvesting, or animal care, learning more about the agricultural way of life.

Cultural Performances: Enjoy the cultural presentations that your hosts have arranged, which include traditional music and dancing. The vibrant exhibits highlight the diverse cultural traditions of the ethnic communities of Ha Giang.

Workshops for Handicrafts: Attend workshops where accomplished craftspeople will instruct you in age-old trades including weaving, needlework, and blacksmithing. Make your own trinkets to bring home.

Photography Opportunities

Golden Rice Terraces: Ha Giang's terraced fields are a photographer's paradise, particularly around the time of planting and harvesting. Mesmerizing sceneries are produced by the golden colors of the maturing rice against the background of lush hills.

Sunrise and Sunset: During the glistening hours of sunrise and sunset, Ha Giang's stunning views are enhanced. Take photos of the mountains, valleys, and interaction of light and shadow.

Vibrant Markets: Ha Giang's regional markets, like those in Meo Vac, Quan Ba, and Dong Van, provide interesting photographic possibilities. The lively scenery, vibrant traditional attire, and expressive faces of the natives create captivating images.

Ethnic Portraits: With the local communities' permission, you may take pictures of members of ethnic minorities. Their uncommon attire and striking facial traits make them compelling photographic subjects.

Natural Wonders: Caves, waterfalls, and lush woods are just a few of the natural beauties that the province is home to. Each one provides endless photography ideas.

Cultural Festivals: If your trip falls during one of the town's festivals, you'll have the opportunity to photograph colorful processions, elaborate costumes, and live performances.

Ha Giang's experiences and activities appeal to a variety of interests, whether you're looking for exhilarating thrills, cultural immersion, or the ideal photograph. Ha Giang offers memorable experiences that you will remember long after you have left this alluring province, like riding a motorcycle on wide roads, hiking distant trails, and dining with local families.

EATING AND DINING

The culinary scene in Ha Giang is a delicious medley of tastes that showcases the area's rich cultural variety and agricultural richness. You may enjoy regional cuisine when eating in this province, which has meals made using local products and prepared using time-honored methods. In this part, we'll discuss some must-try regional cuisine and point you to well-known eateries and cafés where you may eat it.

Local Dishes to Try

Thang Co: A well-known Hmong cuisine, Thang Co is a robust and flavorful stew cooked with a variety of meats, including pig, horse, and buffalo, as well as herbs and spices. This shared meal is often eaten during celebrations and gatherings.

Banh Cuon: Banh Cuon is a Vietnamese dish made of thin rice flour sheets that are stuffed with ground pork, mushrooms, and herbs. It's usually served with a flavorful dipping sauce and makes a great breakfast or snack.

Grilled Specialties: Ha Giang's hilly topography offers many possibilities for grilling, leading to savory delicacies such as grilled fish, bamboo shoots, and pork skewers. Local herbs and spices are often used to season these recipes.

Thit Lon Cap Nach: This unusual delicacy, called Thit Lon Cap Nach, is made using freshly killed pig that is prepared in a variety of ways, such as grilling and stir-frying. It is renowned for both its particular taste and freshness.

Local Herbs & Greens: Ha Giang is home to a variety of wild herbs and greens that are often utilized to improve the taste of food. Try using herbs like "rau que," a spicy herb, or "rau cai," leafy greens, in your recipes.

Bitter Bamboo Shoot Soup (Canh Mang Chua): A delicacy of the area, this acidic and cooling soup is created with fish, young bitter bamboo shoots, and a variety of fragrant herbs. It's a lovely way to sample the regional cuisine.

Popular Restaurants and Cafes

Ngoc Minh Restaurant (Nha Hang Ngoc Minh): Ha Giang City's Ngoc Minh Restaurant is well-known for its broad menu of regional cuisine. Don't pass up the chance to sample Thang Co and other Hmong dishes at this warm restaurant.

Hoa Ban Plus Restaurant: Hoa Ban Plus Restaurant is a well-liked option for tourists and is located in the center of Dong Van Town. It serves a fusion of regional and Vietnamese cuisine, including grilled foods and filling stews.

Hanh Cafe & Coffee: In Ha Giang City, stop at Hanh Cafe for a nice cafe experience. This lovely location offers delicious coffee, cool drinks, and little munchies. It's a nice spot to unwind and make plans for the day.

Quyet Tien Restaurant: Vietnamese traditional cuisine is served in the Quyet Tien

Restaurant, which is close to the Quyet Tien Hot Springs. You may indulge in regional cuisines like grilled fish and stir-fried veggies after taking a soothing bath in the hot springs.

Local Markets: Although they are not conventional restaurants or cafés, Ha Giang's local markets provide a distinctive eating experience. You may taste snacks, fresh veggies, and street cuisine. Don't forget to sample any local vendors' offerings of regional delicacies.

Homestays: You will have the opportunity to eat meals made at home by your hosts while staying in an ethnic minority homestay. These dishes provide a genuine sense of Ha Giang since they often use locally obtained ingredients and traditional techniques.

The gastronomic scene in Ha Giang is a delicious excursion into the core of northern Vietnamese cuisine. Discovering the regional cuisine and dining options in this province not only satisfies your palate but also provides a chance to engage with the culture and friendliness of the locals. Make sure to sample the local delicacies and appreciate the tastes that make Ha Giang a place to indulge in fine dining.

ACCOMMODATION OPTIONS

To guarantee a relaxing and pleasurable trip, it's crucial to choose the ideal accommodation while in Ha Giang. Fortunately, the province has a wide selection of lodging choices to accommodate different needs and interests. We'll examine the several forms of lodging in this part, including hotels, hostels, homestays, and eco-lodges.

Hotels, Hostels, and Guesthouses

Hotels: The provincial capital of Ha Giang City is home to a variety of inns that can be found in a range of price ranges. There are cozy alternatives available with features like Wi-Fi, air conditioning, and private bathrooms. The Huang Anh Hotel and the Ha Giang Hotel are popular options. These provide a practical starting point for discovering the city and its surroundings.

Hostels: If you want to travel on a tight budget or want a more sociable setting, think about staying in hostels. Numerous hostels in Ha Giang City and Dong Van provide both private rooms and dormitory-style accommodations. These are excellent for making new friends and exchanging travel tales. A well-liked option in Dong Van is the Panorama Hostel, which has a rooftop patio with amazing views.

Guesthouses: Located all around Ha Giang Province, guesthouses provide straightforward and reasonably priced lodging. These are often managed by families and provide a friendly environment. Guesthouses are a fantastic choice for tourists on a budget since they often provide tidy rooms with simple facilities. Guesthouses may be found in several cities and villages, including Quan Ba and Meo Vac.

Homestays and Eco-Lodges

Homestays: Among the most immersing and culturally enlightening experiences you can have in Ha Giang is staying in a homestay. Many ethnic minority groups welcome visitors into their homes, allowing them to interact with local families and take part in their everyday routines. In villages all around the province, including those in Quan Ba, Yen Minh, and Dong Van, homestays are offered. You'll stay in traditional homes, eat meals that are prepared at home, and learn about the traditions and customs of your hosts.

Lung Cam Cultural Village: Homestays in conventional Hmong dwellings are available at Lung Cam Cultural Village, which is close to Quan Ba. You may work in the fields, discover Hmong traditions, and take in breathtaking views of the Quan Ba Twin Mountains.

Nam Dam Village: This Tay stilt house guesthouse is located in the Dong Van Karst Plateau Geopark. It's a chance to experience Tay culture fully, discover the geopark, and hike to neighboring sights.

Lung Cu Village: Staying there allows you to interact with the Hmong neighborhood next to the Lung Cu Flag Tower. It's a special opportunity that lets you go to Vietnam's far north.

Eco-Lodges: Ha Giang's eco-lodges are a great option for tourists looking for a place that balances comfort with sustainability. These lodges are often tucked away in picturesque locations, offering a peaceful refuge from the bustle. They often use eco-friendly techniques and provide a variety of conveniences.

Pulse Hill Lodge: The eco-lodge Pulse Hill Lodge, which is close to Quan Ba, provides cozy accommodations with contemporary facilities while maintaining a dedication to sustainability. It's a tranquil retreat among Ha Giang's breathtaking scenery.

Ha Thanh Eco-Lodge: The Ha Thanh Eco-Lodge, located in Ha Giang City, combines contemporary comfort with eco-friendly methods. It's the perfect option for anyone who desires quick access to the city's attractions without sacrificing peace and quiet.

Ban Tuy Homestay & Lodge: This eco-lodge is located in the Ban Tuy Village and mixes homestay experiences with luxurious accommodations. You may work in agriculture, visit the community, and unwind in a natural environment.

You should take your desired experience into account while selecting your Ha Giang lodging. While homestays and eco-lodges provide opportunities for cultural immersion and connection with nature, hotels and hostels give comfort and convenience. Whatever you decide, Ha Giang's friendly residents will make your stay memorable and inviting.

PRACTICAL INFORMATION

There are a few practical things to keep in mind to ensure an easy and pleasurable trip to Ha Giang. To help you make the most of your visit to this beautiful province, we'll present important information on communication and internet access, health and medical services, and sustainable travel habits in this area.

Communication & Internet Access

Mobile Networks: In Ha Giang, the majority of metropolitan areas and key routes should have mobile network coverage. The three largest mobile network operators in Vietnam, Viettel, Vinaphone, and Mobifone, are present in Ha Giang. However, in isolated communities and hilly regions, signal strength may differ.

SIM Cards: If you want to use mobile internet and make calls while you're in Vietnam, it's a good idea to get a Vietnamese SIM card when you get there. In Ha Giang City, SIM cards are readily available in airports, convenience shops, and mobile network retailers.

Internet Access: Although internet connectivity is accessible in Ha Giang, the connection speed in rural regions may be slower. In Ha Giang City, there are a lot of lodging options, hostels, and coffee shops. Be prepared, however, for patchy connections in isolated settlements.

Medical and Health Facilities

Health Precautions: It is advisable to speak with a medical practitioner about the required vaccines and health precautions before visiting Ha Giang. Make sure your usual immunizations are up to date and think about becoming immunized against illnesses like typhoid and hepatitis A, which may be spread via contaminated food and water.

Travel Insurance: It is highly advised that you get comprehensive travel insurance that includes coverage for unexpected medical expenses while visiting Ha Giang. Verify that the popular in the area activities such as riding motorcycles and hiking are covered by your insurance policy.

Pharmacies: You may locate pharmacies in Ha Giang City and bigger towns that provide standard pharmaceuticals and first-aid supplies. It is advised to carry any prescription drugs you need since they may not be accessible where you are.

Medical Facilities: Basic medical facilities are available at the hospital in Ha Giang City. It's crucial to have a strategy in place in case of crises since you may need to go to bigger cities like Hanoi or Lao Cai for more significant medical concerns or emergencies.

Sustainable Travel Practices

Respect Local Culture: The different ethnic minority populations that makeup Ha Giang each have their own traditions and customs. Dress modestly, get permission before taking photographs, and observe any cultural customs that are presented to you throughout your visit to demonstrate respect for the local cultures.

Reduce Plastic Use: Carry a reusable water bottle, and steer clear of single-use plastics to help cut down on plastic waste. By providing free refills of filtered water, several lodgings and cafés in Ha Giang encourage environmentally responsible activities.

Litter Disposal: Get rid of rubbish properly by using the specified containers for litter. Carry out all of your rubbish and leave no evidence of your stay if you're walking through isolated locations or going on vacation there.

Support Local Communities: When making purchases, give local farmers' markets and craftspeople first consideration. Your assistance immediately supports the neighborhood's residents and economy.

Use Local Guides: Consider using local guides while going on a hike or engaging in other activities. They have in-depth local expertise, support the community's economy, and may enrich your experience by sharing their understanding of the local way of life.

Choose Eco-Friendly Accommodations: Select lodgings that adhere to sustainable and eco-friendly principles. Eco-lodges and homestays often take steps to lessen their influence on the environment, such as employing renewable energy sources and cutting down on water use.

Responsible Trekking: Trekking responsibly means staying on well-traveled paths to cause the least amount of environmental harm possible. If you're planning an overnight hike, don't pick flora or spook animals, and only camp in approved places.

Conservation Efforts: Learn about regional conservation efforts and lend your support to groups preserving Ha Giang's natural beauty and cultural legacy.

Responsible Motorbike Riding: If you want to take a motorbike excursion, safety should come first. Wear the proper safety equipment, abide by traffic laws, and be mindful of the state of the roads. Before starting off, make sure your bike is in excellent working order.

You can reduce your environmental footprint and make a positive difference in the communities you visit while traveling sustainably in Ha Giang. Future generations may appreciate the beauty and cultural diversity of the province by respecting local culture, protecting the environment, and putting responsible tourism first.

SAMPLE ITINERARIES

For you to get the most out of your trip to Ha Giang, planning the ideal itinerary is crucial. Ha Giang has a variety of landscapes, lively cultures, and activities to satisfy a range of interests. We'll provide you two suggested itineraries in this section—an exciting 3-day trip and a thorough 7-day tour. We'll also provide advice on how to design personalized itineraries that suit your tastes.

3-Day Ha Giang Adventure

Day 1: Quan Ba and Ha Giang City
- Arrive at Ha Giang City, then settle into the lodging of your choice.
- Explore the city, go to the neighborhood markets, and get familiar with the local way of life.
- In the afternoon, Go to Quan Ba District to see the recognizable Quan Ba Twin Mountains. To learn about the Hmong and Dao cultures, visit the adjacent villages.

- Spend the night in Quan Ba in a homestay or small guesthouse.

Day 2: Dong Van Karst Plateau Geopark
- Set off towards Dong Van while traversing the breathtaking Ma Pi Leng Pass. Spectacular views of the Nho Que River below are available.
- Discover the Dong Van Old Quarter, which has French colonial architecture, and the Dong Van Karst Plateau Geopark.
- Visit the Lung Cu Flag Tower, which marks Vietnam's northernmost point.
- Spend the night at a hostel or guesthouse in Dong Van.

Day 3: Meo Vac and return to Ha Giang City
- Travel to Meo Vac, a town renowned for its lively markets and beautiful surroundings.
- Explore the Meo Vac Market (if you go on a Sunday, you'll see a busy ethnic market there).
- After lunch, Make your way back to Ha Giang City.

- Finish your trip at Ha Giang City, where you may take a moment to consider your experience and eat at a local restaurant.

7-Day Ha Giang Exploration

Day 1: Ha Giang City
- Start your adventure at Ha Giang City and familiarize yourself with the region. Discover the marketplaces and sights of the city.

Day 2: Quan Ba and Yen Minh
- As you go to Quan Ba, pause to take in the twin mountains of Quan Ba.
- Visit the villages of Quan Ba and engage with the Hmong and Dao populations there.
- Continue to Yen Minh where you will spend the night.

Day 3: Dong Van and Surroundings
- Trek to neighboring sights while visiting the Lung Cam Cultural Village.
- Learn about the history of Dong Van Old Quarter by exploring it.

- Spend the night at Dong Van.

Day 4: Ma Pi Leng Pass and Meo Vac
- Set out on the renowned Ma Pi Leng Pass trip while snapping breath-blowing pictures.
- Get to Meo Vac, look around its ethnic marketplaces, and talk to the people there.
- Sleepover at Meo Vac.

Day 5: Lung Cu and Cultural Experiences
- Visit Vietnam's northernmost point, the Lung Cu Flag Tower.
- Enjoy cultural interactions while exploring other ethnic settlements.
- Return to Dong Van for the evening.

Day 6: Bao Lac and Off-the-Beaten-Path Villages
- Travel to Bao Lac, a quaint hamlet renowned for the variety of ethnic communities who call it home.
- Explore remote settlements and take part in unique cultural encounters.
- Sleep in Bao Lac.

Day 7: Go back to Ha Giang City
- Go back to Ha Giang City to finish your adventure with a supper at a neighborhood eatery.
- Consider your seven-day journey across the many areas and cultures of Ha Giang.

Suggestions for Customized Itineraries

Ha Giang provides a wide variety of customizable tour alternatives for visitors with particular interests:

Trekking & Hiking: Extend your stay by taking part in multi-day treks through far-flung settlements and scenic surroundings.

Photography Focus: Spend more time in popular locations during the best light of dawn and sunset.

Cultural Immersion: Extend your stay in houses of ethnic minorities to get a deeper comprehension of the cultures there.

Motorbike Expeditions: Customize your route for a motorcycle expedition to visit undiscovered communities and outlying roads that suit your riding style and interests.

Off-Beaten-Path Exploration: Take extra days to explore isolated natural beauties and undiscovered treasures.

Ha Giang's adaptability enables you to design a schedule that fits your interests and time constraints. Ha Giang is ready to be explored and personalized to your interests, whether you're looking for adventure, cultural experiences, or a mix of both.

GETTING TO KNOW THE LOCALS

A visit to Ha Giang involves more than simply taking in the gorgeous scenery; it also involves getting to know the many different ethnic cultures who live here. Your travel experience may be enhanced while making a good contribution to the communities you visit by getting to know the inhabitants, exploring their customs, and participating in responsible tourism projects.

Meeting the Ethnic Communities of Ha Giang

With Hmong, Dao, Tay, and several more ethnic groups dwelling in the area, Ha Giang is recognized for its ethnic variety. How to interact with these communities is as follows:

Homestays: Spending time in people's homes is one of the finest ways to get to know them. In

Ha Giang, there are several opportunities for homestays that provide you the opportunity to live with Hmong, Tay, and Dao households. You'll participate in everyday activities with them, have meals with them, and learn about their way of life.

Cultural Workshops: A few towns provide cultural workshops where you may learn how to make things like blacksmithing, weaving, and embroidery. These workshops provide practical training and the chance to speak with regional craftspeople.

Local Markets: Visit the thriving local markets in cities like Meo Vac, Quan Ba, and Dong Van. You may see everyday life, enjoy regional cuisine, and buy handcrafted goods at these ethnic groups' meeting spots.

Festivals & Celebrations: If your trip falls during one of the town's festivals, take advantage of the opportunity to take part. These festivals often include vibrant parades, music, dancing, and traditional clothing, providing a peek into Ha Giang's diverse cultural heritage.

Ritual Participation: You may be able to take part in rituals and ceremonies with the assistance of the locals. These encounters provide light on the community's spiritual and cultural values.

Language & Communication: Although English is not commonly spoken in Ha Giang, knowing a few fundamental words can help you build relationships and respect for the local way of life.

Initiatives for Responsible Travel

To practice responsible tourism, visitors must interact positively with the local population and the environment. Ha Giang has adopted several programs to encourage ethical travel, including:

Community-Based Tourism (CBT): Several villages in Ha Giang have embraced CBT strategies, which include the local population in tourism-related activities. Direct financial assistance is provided to the community and its citizens via homestays, guided tours, and cultural events.

Eco-Friendly Practices: Eco-friendly techniques are prioritized by several eco-lodges and lodgings in Ha Giang. These efforts include water conservation, trash reduction, and the utilization of renewable energy sources.

Local Guides: Hiring local guides for outdoor activities like hiking improves your experience while also giving local people and communities a source of income. These guides have in-depth local knowledge and may encourage cordial contact with locals.

Responsible Trekking: In Ha Giang, trekking associations and tour providers often instruct trekkers on proper conduct. This entails respecting the environment, abiding by designated paths, and reducing trash.

Supporting Local Artisans: Buying directly from local craftsmen at markets or workshops helps to support their livelihoods and preserves traditional crafts. This is known as "Supporting Local Artisans."

Preserving Cultural Heritage: Various local projects and organizations aim to protect and promote the cultural legacy of Ha Giang's ethnic minority populations. Participate in cultural events and adhere to cultural customs to support their efforts.

Educational Programs: Some localities provide educational opportunities for visitors to learn about customs, agriculture, and sustainable lifestyle choices. These initiatives promote understanding and foster cross-cultural interaction.

By taking part in these projects for responsible tourism and interacting with the local communities in Ha Giang, you not only improve your vacation experience but also actively support the economic prosperity of the locals you encounter. The friendly locals of Ha Giang are ready to share their customs, historical tales, and gracious hospitality with tourists who treat the area with respect and dedication to responsible tourism.

CONCLUSION

It's time to reflect on the remarkable experience that awaits you in this distant and alluring province of Vietnam as we come to the end of our Ha Giang travel guide for 2023.

Ha Giang is a place unlike any other because of its striking scenery, diverse cultural heritage, and friendly people. Every second in Ha Giang is a brushstroke of natural grandeur, from the soaring peaks of the Dong Van Karst Plateau Geopark to the peaceful serenity of the terraced rice fields.

We've covered everything you need to know to plan your vacation in this guide, from the ideal times to visit and visa requirements to lodging choices, activities, and responsible tourism principles. We looked into the must-see sights, little-known attractions, and the tastes of Ha Giang's delectable food. Ha Giang offers it all, whether you're looking for soul-soothing hikes, heart-racing motorcycle rides, or in-depth cultural encounters.

You may start your vacation with one of our recommended itineraries, which includes a 3-day adventure and a 7-day excursion. Nevertheless, Ha Giang's adaptability enables you to customize your trip to your interests, regardless of whether you're an enthusiastic tourist, a photographer, or a culture buff.

Keep in mind the value of responsible tourism as you set out on your Ha Giang excursion. Participate in local communities, observe their traditions, and make a good impact everywhere you go. By doing this, you'll contribute to the sustainability of this amazing province and make lifelong memories.

Your heart and spirit will carry an imprint of Ha Giang forever. It is a place where only the kindness of its people can compete with the untamed beauty of nature. Ha Giang provides opportunities for deep connection and learning, whether you're admiring the magnificent Quan Ba Twin Mountains, enjoying a bowl of Thang

Co stew with new acquaintances, or exchanging tales over a homestay fire.

So be ready for the experience of a lifetime and pack your things before setting off for Ha Giang. Allow Ha Giang's tranquil scenery, meandering mountain roads, and neighborhood kids' laughing to lead you to a place of wonder and inspiration.

I wish you a memorable journey in Ha Giang, rich cultural encounters, and a profound appreciation for the beauty of the natural world. The adventurous tourist is yearning to discover the hidden beauties and vivid traditions of Ha Giang Province. Welcome to Ha Giang, a city filled with enchantment and adventure around every turn.

APPENDIX

Glossary of Local Terms

Hmong: One of the ethnic minorities of Ha Giang is the Hmong, who are renowned for their distinctive traditions and brightly colored traditional attire.

Dao: A well-known ethnic minority in the province, distinguished by their red turbans and extensive cultural traditions.

Tay: An ethnic group in the area distinguished by its stilt homes and agricultural methods.

Quan Ba Twin Mountains: Also known as "Twin Mountain" or "Heaven's Gate," are a representation of the splendor of Ha Giang's landscape.

Ma Pi Leng Pass: A stunning mountain pass known for its sheer cliffs and expansive vistas is called Ma Pi Leng Pass.

Dong Van Karst Plateau Geopark: A geopark designated by UNESCO, the Dong Van Karst Plateau Geopark is home to beautiful limestone structures and a distinctive geological past.

Lung Cu Flag Tower: Vietnamese sovereignty is symbolized by the Lung Cu Flag Tower, which is situated at the country's most northern point.

Thang Co: A traditional Hmong stew that often includes a variety of meats and seasonings.

Useful Vietnamese Phrases

- Hello: Xin chào (sin chow)
- Thank you: Cảm ơn (kahm uhn)
- Yes: Vâng (vang)
- No: Không (kh-uh-ng)
- Please: Xin vui lòng (sin vooi luong)
- Excuse me / Sorry: Xin lỗi (sin loi)
- How much is this?: Bao nhiêu tiền? (bow nhyoo ty-en?)
- Where is...?: ...ở đâu? (...uh dhow?)

- I don't understand: Tôi không hiểu (toy kh-uh-ng hy-uh-ooh)
- Help: Giúp đỡ (z-yoop doh)
- Water: Nước (nwahk)
- Food: Thức ăn (toog uhn)
- Restroom: Nhà vệ sinh (nya vay sin)
- I'm lost: Tôi bị lạc đường (toy bee l-uh-k doong)
- Goodbye: Tạm biệt (tahm byet)

Your interactions with locals will be considerably improved and your trip to Ha Giang will be more pleasurable if you learn a few simple Vietnamese words. It demonstrates respect for the local way of life and might result in enduring bonds with the people you come across.

Printed in Great Britain
by Amazon